Romans

Good News
that Changes
Everything

LEADER GUIDE

A Bible Study by

MELISSA SPOELSTRA

Abingdon Women
Nashville

Romans
Good News that Changes Everything
Leader Guide

ISBN 978-1-5018-3899-6

19 20 21 22 23 24 25 26 27 28—10 9 8 7 6 5 4 3 2 1
MANUFACTURED IN THE UNITED STATES OF AMERICA

Contents

About the Author

Melissa Spoelstra is a popular women's conference speaker (including the Aspire Tour), Bible teacher, and author who is madly in love with Jesus and passionate about studying God's Word and helping women of all ages seek Christ and know Him more intimately through serious Bible study. Having a degree in Bible theology, she enjoys teaching God's Word to the body of Christ, traveling to diverse groups and churches across the United States and also to Nairobi, Kenya, for a women's prayer conference. Melissa is the author of the Bible studies *Elijah: Spiritual Stamina in Every Season*, *Numbers: Learning Contentment in a Culture of More*, *First Corinthians: Living Love When We Disagree*, *Joseph: The Journey to Forgiveness*, and *Jeremiah: Daring to Hope in an Unstable World* and the books *Dare to Hope: Living Intentionally in an Unstable World*, *Total Family Makeover: 8 Practical Steps to Making Disciples at Home*, and *Total Christmas Makeover: 31 Devotions to Celebrate with Purpose*. She is a regular contributor to the Proverbs 31 First Five App and the Girlfriends in God online daily devotional. She has published articles in *ParentLife*, *Women's Spectrum*, and *Just Between Us* and writes her own regular blog in which she shares her musings about what God is teaching her on any given day. Melissa lives in Pickerington, Ohio, with her pastor husband, Sean, and their four kids: Zach, Abby, Sara, and Rachel.

Follow Melissa:

 Twitter @MelSpoelstra

 Instagram @Daring2Hope

 Facebook @AuthorMelissaSpoelstra

Her blog   MelissaSpoelstra.com (check here also for event dates and booking information)

Introduction

While bad news surrounds us, the Letter to the Romans reminds us of good news. Although we were separated from God when sin entered the world, we can find a restored relationship with God through His Son, Jesus Christ. Jesus sacrificed His life as the payment for sin and rose again from the dead. When we confess with our mouths and believe in our hearts the message about Christ, we are saved from the penalty, power, and eventually the very presence of sin. This is good news that has the power to change everything in our lives.

The apostle Paul penned this letter to the church at Rome. Early church fathers and leaders of movements of spiritual revival often credit the good news in Romans as being pivotal in great works of God throughout history. The truths found in Romans continue to help us understand our relationship with our Creator today. In our study, we'll find that faith is central to following Christ.

Romans is full of both doctrine and practical truths. By studying the context and historical background with the participants in your group and then making personal application, I believe you will see God at work in your own lives and the lives of those around you.

Over the next six weeks we'll encounter good news in the following areas:

1. faith
2. hope
3. daily life
4. God's plan
5. relationships
6. eternity

Together we'll see that even if bad news is coming at us from every direction, we can hold fast to the good news. Our God is with us. He loves us and has a plan for us. This good news informs our identity as those dearly loved by God and impacts our daily lives and relationships. It has the power to change everything in our lives here on earth and brings hope for the next. The truths in Romans are powerful and echo into eternity!

About the Participant Workbook

Before the first session, you will want to distribute copies of the participant workbook *Romans: Good News that Changes Everything* to the members of your group. Be sure to communicate that they are to complete the first week of readings *before* your session for Week 1. (If you plan to have an Introductory Session, they will begin the homework after that.) For each week, there are five readings or lessons that combine study of Scripture with personal reflection and application (**boldface type** indicates write-in-the-book questions and activities). Each lesson ends with a "Talk with God" prayer suggestion.

On average you will need about twenty to thirty minutes for each lesson. Completing these readings each week will prepare the women for the discussion and activities of the group session.

About This Leader Guide

As you gather each week with the members of your group, you will have the opportunity to watch a video, discuss and respond to what you're learning, and pray together. You will need access to a television and DVD player with working remotes. (Or if you prefer, you may purchase streaming video files at www.Cokesbury.com.)

Creating a warm and inviting atmosphere will help make the women feel welcome. Although optional, you might consider providing snacks for your first meeting and inviting group members to rotate in bringing refreshments each week.

This Leader Guide and the video will be your primary tools for leading your group on this journey to learn how to have spiritual stamina. Whether you choose to follow this guide step by step, modify its contents to meet your group's needs and preferences, or simply peruse it to find a few helpful tips, questions, and ideas, you will find in these pages some valuable tools for creating a successful group experience.

> **Getting Started:** This is a list of strategies, options, and introductory information that will help you ensure good organization and com- munication. You will want to review this material and communicate

relevant information to group members prior to your group session for Week 1, either via email or in an introductory session (see more about this in "Getting Started"). Or you might consider adding fifteen to thirty minutes to your first session for reviewing some of these important housekeeping details. Whichever option you choose, be sure group members have the opportunity to purchase workbooks and complete Week 1 before your session for Week 1.

Tips for Tackling Five Common Challenges: This section includes ideas for addressing recurring issues that come up when leading a group. Every leader knows that some group dynamics can be difficult to tackle. What will you do when one person dominates the discussion or cuts off another person who is speaking? All eyes will be on you to see how you will intervene or ignore these situations. Be sure to check out these five common challenges and ideas to help when you encounter them.

Basic Leader Helps: This list of basic leader tips will help you to prepare for and lead each group session.

Session Outlines: Six adaptable outlines are provided to help guide your group time each week. Each begins with a "Leader Prep" section to assist with preparation.

Digging Deeper Articles: At the end of this book, you'll find a preview of one of the "Digging Deeper" articles that are available online at AbingdonWomen.com/Romans. In these articles you will find second-level, concise information your group members do not have in their participant workbooks, such as cultural insights, background information, commentary, and so forth. (You're encouraged to read the full articles online prior to your group session.) As you dialogue with God about leading each session, ask Him what parts of the corresponding "Digging Deeper" article He might want you to share with the group. This will give participants an opportunity to continue to learn new insights in your time together each week. Feel free to point your group members to the online articles in class or via email or social media. One thing I've found helpful is to allow women to sign up to read an article ahead of time and then share a few insights they gained from it with the group.

This study is designed for six weeks, with an optional introductory session. Or, if desired, you may choose to extend the study to eight or twelve weeks; see the options included in "Getting Started." Again, whichever option you choose, be sure that group members have the opportunity to purchase participant workbooks and complete Week 1 before your session for Week 1.

Each of the session outlines in this book may be used for a 60-minute, 90-minute, or 120-minute session. The following formats are offered as templates that you may modify for your group:

60-Minute Format

Welcome/Fellowship (2 minutes)
All Play (3–5 minutes)
Prayer/Video (25–30 minutes)
Group Discussion (20 minutes)
Prayer Requests (3 minutes)

90-Minute Format

Welcome/Fellowship (5–10 minutes)
All Play (3–5 minutes)
Prayer/Video (25–30 minutes)
Group Discussion (25 minutes)
Optional "Digging Deeper" Summary (2–3 minutes)
Optional Group Activity (5–10 minutes)
Prayer Requests (5 minutes)

120-Minute Format

Welcome/Fellowship (10–12 minutes)
All Play (5–10 minutes)
Prayer/Video (25–30 minutes)
Group Discussion (30–35 minutes)
Optional "Digging Deeper" Summary (2–3 minutes)
Optional Group Activity (10 minutes)
Prayer Requests (15–20 minutes)

As you can see, the basic elements remain the same in each format: a welcome/fellowship time, an "All Play" icebreaker question that everyone can answer, an opportunity to share insights with the group from the week's "Digging Deeper" article, a video segment, group discussion, and prayer time. The 90-minute and 120-minute options offer longer times for fellowship, discussion, and prayer plus an optional group activity. If you choose not to do the group activity, you may add that time to another element of the session, such as group discussion or prayer. (See "Getting Started" for notes about including food, planning for childcare, and other important organizational details.)

If you are new to leading Bible studies and/or would like to have a framework to follow, the session outlines will guide you. Note that more discussion questions have been provided than you may have time to include. Before the session, choose the questions you want to cover and put a check mark beside them. Page references are provided for those questions that relate to questions or activities in the participant workbook. For these questions, invite group members to turn in their participant workbooks to the pages indicated.

If you are a seasoned group leader looking only for a few good questions or ideas, I encourage you to take what you want and leave the rest. After all, you know your group better than I do! Ask God to show you what areas to focus on from the week's homework and use my discussion outline as a template that you can revise.

Of course, the Holy Spirit knows the content of this study (His Word) and the women in your group better than anyone, so above all I encourage you to lead this study under the Holy Spirit's direction, allowing yourself the freedom to make any changes or adaptations that are helpful or desirable.

I'm so excited that God has called you to lead a group of ladies through a study of Romans. Know that I am praying for you and believing God for the work He will do through your leadership. Now, let's get started!

Melissa

Getting Started

Before your study begins, be sure to review the following introductory information that will help you ensure good organization and communication. You are encouraged to communicate relevant information such as the dates, times, and location for group meetings; when/where/how to purchase workbooks; details regarding childcare and food; expectations and ground rules; and an overview of the study to group members during an introductory session or via email before your session for Week 1.

1. Determine the length of your study. The basic study is designed for six weeks (plus an optional introductory session), but you also can plan for an eight- or twelve-week study.

   - **For a six-week study**—plus an additional (optional) introductory session if desired—use the session guides in this book and the video segments (DVD or streaming files). Be sure to distribute workbooks during the introductory session if you are having one or prior to your session for Week 1.

   - **For an eight-week study**, add both an introductory session and a closing celebration. In the introductory session, watch the introductory video message and spend time getting to know one another, presenting basic housekeeping information, and praying together (use the guide on page 25 in the Leader Guide). For a closing celebration, discuss what you have learned together in a special gathering that includes refreshments or perhaps a brunch, luncheon, or supper. A closing celebration provides an excellent opportunity for ongoing groups to invite friends and reach out to others who might be interested in joining the group for a future study.

- **For a twelve-week study**, you will allow more time for completing homework. This is especially helpful for groups with mothers of young children or women carrying a heavy work or ministry schedule. With this option, women have two weeks in which to complete each week of homework in the participant workbook. In your group sessions, watch and discuss the video the first week; then review and discuss homework the next week. Some women find they are better able to complete assignments and digest what they are learning this way.

2. Determine the length of each group session (60, 90, or 120 minutes). See the format templates outlined on page 8 in the Leader Guide.

3. Decide ahead of time if you/your church will purchase participant workbooks that group members can buy in advance during an introductory session or in advance of your first session, or if group members will buy their own workbooks individually. If you expect each member to buy her own workbook, email group members purchasing information (be sure to note the cost, including tax and shipping if applicable). Consider including online links as well. Be sure to allow enough time for participants to purchase workbooks and complete the readings for Week 1 prior to your session for Week 1.

4. Create a group roster that includes each group member's name, email, mailing address, and primary phone number. (Collect this information through registration, email, or an introductory session.) Distribute copies of the roster to group members prior to or during your first session. A group roster enables group members to stay connected and contact one another freely as needed, such as when taking a meal or sending a card to someone who is sick, who has missed several group sessions, or who has had a baby or another significant life event. Group members may want to meet for coffee or lunch to follow up on things shared in the study as well. As women cry and laugh and share life together in a Bible study, their lives will be intertwined, even if for a short time.

5. Make decisions about childcare and food and communicate this information to group members in advance. Will childcare be offered, and will there be a cost associated with it? Will refreshments be served at your gatherings? (Note: If your group is meeting for 60 minutes, you will not have time for a formal fellowship time with refreshments. You might consider having refreshments set up early

and inviting women to come a few minutes before the session officially begins.) If you choose to have food, the introductory meeting is a good time to pass around a sign-up sheet. In the Bible study group I lead, we like to eat, so we have three women sign up to bring food for each meeting. One brings fruit, another brings bread or muffins, and another brings an egg dish. Your group may want to keep it simple; just be mindful of food allergies and provide choices.

6. Let group members know what to expect. Those who have never participated in a women's Bible study group may be intimidated, scared, or unsure of what to expect. Friends have told me that when they first came to Bible study, they were concerned they would be called on to pray out loud or expected to know everything in the Bible. Ease group members' concerns up front. Reassure the women that they will not be put on the spot and that they may choose to share as they are comfortable. Encourage participation while fostering a "safe" environment. Laying a few basic ground rules such as these can help you achieve this kind of environment:

    *   *Confidentiality*. Communicate that anything shared in the group is not to be repeated outside of those present in the study. Women need to feel safe to be vulnerable and authentic.

    *   *Sensitivity*. Talk about courtesy, which includes practices such as refraining from interrupting, monopolizing, or trying to "fix" shared problems. Women want to be heard, not told what to do, when they share an issue in their lives. If they have advice to share with an individual, ask them to speak with the person privately after study. When studying God's Word, some differences of opinion are bound to arise as to interpretation and/or application. This is a good place to sharpen one another and respectfully disagree so that you may grow and understand different viewpoints. Remind the women that it's okay to question and see things differently; however, they must be kind and sensitive to the feelings of others.

    *   *Purpose*. The primary reason you are taking time out of your busy schedules to meet together is to study the Bible. Though your group will pray for, serve, and support one another, your primary focus is to study the Bible. You learn in community from one another as you draw near to God through His Word. Though you may want to plan a service or social activity during the course of

your study, these times should be secondary to your study time together. If group members express a desire for the group to do more outreach, service, or socials, gently remind them of the primary reason you gather.

7. Before the study begins, provide a short preview of the study's content, summarizing highlights in an email or introductory session. You might whet the appetite for what is to come by sharing (or reading) parts of the introduction from the participant workbook. Consider sharing a personal story that relates to the study's theme. How is the good news about Jesus giving you perspective in some area of your life? How has the gospel message changed everything in your life? As you are enthusiastic about getting into God's Word together, your members will catch your contagious desire to see how the good news about Jesus resonates in their lives.

8. If you are having an introductory session, show the introductory video and open the floor for women to share in response to the questions on page 26 in the Leader Guide.

9. Be sure to communicate to participants that they are to read Week 1 in the participant workbook prior to your session for Week 1. Review the options for study found in the introduction to the participant workbook and encourage participants to choose the options they plan to complete and then share this information with someone in the group for accountability.

Tips for Tackling Five Common Challenges

Challenge #1: Preparation

Do you know that feeling when Bible study is in two days and you haven't even finished the homework, much less prepared for the group session? We've all been there. When I'm unprepared, I can sense the difference when I'm teaching Sunday school, leading VBS, or facilitating discussion in my women's Bible study group. I'm hurried, scattered, and less confident when I haven't dedicated the proper time for preparation. It doesn't take hours, but it does take commitment.

I check myself with a little acronym when I prepare to lead: S-S-S. Many years ago I was asked to lead a segment on teacher training for a group of VBS leaders. I remember asking the Lord, "What are the most important things to remember when we handle your Word to teach?" As I sat listening, He gave me this process of S-S-S that has stuck with me through the years. It looks like this:

S — Savior. Know your Savior. We must spend time talking, listening, and staying closely connected with Jesus in order to lead well. As we intentionally keep our walk with Him close and vibrant, we can then hear His voice about how to structure our lesson, what questions to ask, and which verses in His Word to focus on.

S — Story. Know your story. Though God has been gracious to me when I've winged it, I feel the most freedom with God's truth when I've prepared thoroughly. Try not to cram in multiple days of homework at one time. Let it sink into your soul by reading curiously and slowly.

Go back to areas that especially strike you and allow God to use His Word in your heart and mind so that you can teach with authenticity. Women can tell when you're flying by the seat of your pants.

S — Students. Know your students. Who are these women God has given you to shepherd? Are they struggling with finances, relationships, or body image issues? Are they mature Christ-followers who need to be challenged to go deeper in their study of God's Word or seekers who need extra explanations about where the books of the Bible are located? Most likely, you will be teaching to a wide range of backgrounds as well as emotional and spiritual maturity levels, and you will need God's wisdom and guidance to inspire them.

Challenge #2: Group Dynamics

Have you experienced that uncomfortable feeling when you ask a discussion question and a long silence settles over the group? With your eyes begging someone to break the ice, you wonder if you should let the question linger or jump in with your own answer. Other problems with group dynamics surface when Silent Suzy never contributes to the conversation because Talking Tammy answers every question. What does a good leader do in these situations? While every group has a unique vibe, I have found these general concepts very helpful in facilitating discussion:

First of all, a good leader asks questions. Jesus was our greatest example. He definitely taught spiritual truths, but one of His most effective methods was asking questions. Proverbs 20:5 says, "Though good advice lies deep within the heart, / a person with understanding will draw it out." As leaders, we must be intentional askers and listeners. I try to gauge myself throughout the discussion by reflecting often on this simple question: "Am I doing all the talking?" When I find I am hearing my own voice too much, I make a point to ask and listen more. Even if waiting means a little silence hangs in the air, eventually someone will pipe up and share. Women learn from each other's insights and experiences; we rob them of others' comments when we monopolize as leaders.

Now what about Talking Tammy? She not only answers every question but also makes a comment after each woman shares something (often relating to one of her own experiences). Try one of these transitional statements:

- "Thanks Tammy, let's see if someone else has some insight as well."
- "Let's hear from someone who hasn't shared yet today."

- "Is there anyone who hasn't talked much today who would be willing to answer this question?"

The hope is that Talking Tammy will realize that she has had a lot of floor time. Sometimes Talking Tammy also struggles to "land the plane." She can't find a stopping place in her story. Help her out by jumping in when she takes a breath and make a summary statement for her. For example, "I hear you saying that you could relate to a need for good news in the midst of all the challenging things in your life. Does anyone else find the good news about Christ resonating in a similar way?" Occasionally I have had to take someone aside in a loving way and address her amount of talking. Pray hard and be gentle, but address the issue. As a leader, you must keep in mind the good of the group as a whole.

I once had several ladies leave the group because they were so frustrated by the continual barrage of talking by one woman in particular. Some of her many comments were insensitive and offensive to others in the room. I don't like confrontation, so I didn't want to address it. However, God grew me as a leader to speak loving truth even when it hurts for the benefit of those we are called to shepherd.

Sometimes even more challenging than Talking Tammy is Silent Suzy. We must walk a fine line as leaders, not putting on the spot those women who are uncomfortable talking in front of others. I have scared women away by being too direct. So how do we get Silent Suzy to talk without singling her out? Here are some ideas:

- If she is new to the study, don't push her at all during the first few sessions. Let her feel safe and get comfortable. Never call on her to pray out loud or single her out with a pointed question. I once said, "I want to know what Suzy thinks about this." All eyes turned on her, and I'll never forget the tears welling in the corners of her eyes as she said she wasn't comfortable being called on. She didn't come back to the group after that incident. How I wish I could have taken those words back. I learned a valuable lesson from that Silent Suzy—don't push!
- Listen with recall as she answers the All Play question that everyone is asked to answer. Watch for an opportunity to talk about something she has shared with a follow-up question that doesn't pry.
- Take her out for coffee and get to know her. With time, she might warm up and begin to contribute to the discussion. Through a deepened relationship, you'll get a better read on whether you should encourage her to talk.

Challenge #3: Prayer Requests

How often do we run out of time when sharing prayer requests, leaving us no time to actually pray? How do you handle those women who aren't comfortable praying out loud? What if your group has fifteen to thirty women, and just listening to everyone's prayer request takes half an hour?

It's so important to take the time to hear what is going on in each other's lives and to pray for one another. Here are some creative ideas I have learned from others to help keep prayer time fresh:

- As women enter the room, direct them to take an index card or sticky note and write their prayer request on it. Then during prayer time, each woman can read her request aloud, already having thought through it, and pass it to the woman on the right for her to keep in her Bible as a reminder to pray for the request until they meet again.
- Ask someone to record all the prayer requests and email them to the group each week.
- If you have a small group, use a one- or two-minute sand timer when you are short on time. (Look in your game closet for one of these.) Lightheartedly tell each woman that she has one or two minutes to share her request so that each woman can have a turn. (You might want to flip it over again if tears accompany the request.)
- If you have more than ten women, divide into two or three groups for prayer time. Assign a leader who will facilitate, keep the group on track, and follow up. Sometimes our prayer group has gone out for breakfast together or gathered in someone's home to watch the teaching video again.
- Have women pick one or two partners and split into small groups of two or three to share prayer requests and pray for each other.
- Have an open time of popcorn prayer. This means let women spontaneously pray one-sentence prayers as they feel led.
- After everyone shares requests, ask each woman to pray for the woman on her right. Clearly say that if anyone is uncomfortable praying out loud, she can pray silently and then squeeze the hand of the woman next to her.
- Another option is to close the group in prayer yourself or ask a few women you know are comfortable praying in front of others to pray for the requests mentioned. Remember that many women feel awkward praying in front of others. Provide encouragement by reminding the

group that prayer is talking to God and that there is no right or wrong way to have a conversation with our Creator. But always be sensitive to others and affirm that they will not be looked down on if they don't like to pray out loud.

Making a change in your prayer time occasionally keeps it from becoming routine or boring. Talking with Jesus should be fresh and real. Taking an intentional, thoughtful approach to this important time of your study will add great value to your time together.

Challenge #4: Developing Leaders

Women's Bible study groups are a great avenue for fulfilling the 2-2-2 principle, which comes from 2 Timothy 2:2:

You have heard me teach things that have been confirmed by many reliable witnesses. Now teach these truths to other trustworthy people who will be able to pass them on to others.

As a leader, God calls us to help raise up other leaders.

Is there a woman in your group who is capable of leading? How can you come alongside her and help equip her to be an even better leader? Wonderful women have invested in me through the 2-2-2 principle, even before I knew that term. As an apprentice, I watched them lead. They gave me opportunities to try leading without handing the full reins over to me. Then they coached and corrected me. I have since had the privilege of mentoring several apprentices in my Bible study group and watching them go on to lead their own groups. This is multiplying leaders and groups, and God loves it!

Here is the 2-2-2 principle as laid out by Dave and Jon Ferguson in their book *Exponential*.[1] (My notes are added within brackets.)

- I DO. You WATCH. We TALK.
- I DO. You HELP. We TALK. [Have your apprentice lead a prayer group or an activity or portion of the session.]
- You DO. I HELP. We TALK. [Ask your apprentice to lead one session with you assisting with facilitation alongside her.]
- You DO. I WATCH. We TALK. [Give your apprentice full ownership for leading a session and resist the urge to jump in and take over.]

---

1.   Dave and Jon Ferguson, *Exponential: How You and Your Friends Can Start a Missional Church Movement* (Grand Rapids, MI: Zondervan, 2010), 58, 63-64.

- You DO. Someone else WATCHES. [As God leads over time, encourage your apprentice to start her own Bible study group.]

My mentor and I led a Bible study group together for years. As the group grew larger, we both sensed God leading us to multiply the group, forming two groups. It was painful as we missed studying and working with each other. However, God blessed and used both groups to reach more women. Then a woman in my group felt called to lead her own study. She worried that no one would come to her group. She asked many questions as we worked through the 2-2-2 principle. Her first group meeting included eighteen women who now, five years later, still love meeting together. I've seen pictures of them on Facebook enjoying special times together, and I praise God for all that He is doing.

From our one study there are now over five groups of women that meet regularly to study God's Word. This kind of growth begins with commitment to share leadership, follow the 2-2-2 principle, and multiply so that more women can grow in their walk with Christ. Don't miss the opportunity to develop new leaders with intentionality as you model and encourage other women to use their gifts.

Challenge #5: Reaching Out

How do you welcome new women into the group? This is especially tough if yours is an ongoing group that has had the same women in it for years. Newcomers can feel like outsiders if it seems like everyone already knows the unspoken rules of the group. Also, what about those who are finding their way back to God? Are they welcome in the group? While the purpose of the group is primarily Bible study, I've seen the Great Commission of making disciples happen many times through women's groups that meet for Bible study. God's Word will do the transforming work in their lives through the Holy Spirit. We are called to reach out by investing and inviting. Here are some ways a leader can help create an open group:

- End each Bible study with a closing celebration brunch, encouraging the women to bring food and friends. Some ideas for this time together include:
    1. Have an open time when women can share how God worked in their lives through the Bible study.

2. Have one woman in the group share her testimony of how she came to understand the gospel and how it has been transforming her life recently.
3. Bring in a speaker from outside the group to share a testimony.
4. Make it fun! We play a fun group game (such as Fishbowl, Pictionary, or Loaded Questions) and have a white elephant jewelry exchange at Christmas. Women who might think Bible study is a foreign concept can see that you are just a bunch of regular women in pursuit of a supernatural God.

- Leave an empty chair in the group and pray for God to show you someone who needs a group of women she can study the Bible alongside.
- Though the main purpose of the group is Bible study, consider doing a service project together that you can invite other women to participate in (schedules permitting). Our group has made personal care bags for the homeless and also adopted a family at Christmas, which included going shopping for the gifts and wrapping them together. Depending on where God is leading your group, serving together can help put hands and feet to the truths you are learning.
- Socials outside of Bible study also provide an opportunity to invite friends as a nonthreatening transition. While the focus of your group is much more than social, planning an occasional social event can be a good way to forge deeper connections. Our Bible study group has gone bowling together, had a backyard barbecue, and planned a girls' night out at a local restaurant. These times together not only help women get to know one another better but also give them a great chance to invite friends. These same friends who attend a social might later try a Bible study session once they have made connections with some of the women in the group.

Basic Leader Helps

Preparing for the Sessions

- Check out your meeting space before each group session. Make sure the room is ready. Do you have enough chairs? Do you have the equipment and supplies you need? (See the list of materials needed in each session outline.)
- Pray for your group and each group member by name. Ask God to work in the life of every woman in your group.
- Read and complete the week's readings in the participant workbook, review the session outline in the Leader Guide, and read the "Digging Deeper" article for the week. Put a check mark beside the discussion questions you want to cover and make any notes in the margins that you want to share in your discussion time.

Leading the Sessions

- Personally greet each woman as she arrives. If desired, take attendance using your group roster. (This will assist you in identifying members who have missed several sessions so that you may contact them and let them know they were missed.)
- At the start of each session, ask the women to turn off or silence their cell phones.
- Always start on time. Honor the efforts of those who are on time.
- Encourage everyone to participate fully, but don't put anyone on the spot. Invite the women to share as they are comfortable. Be prepared to offer a personal example or answer if no one else responds at first.
- Facilitate but don't dominate. Remember that if you talk most of

the time, group members may tend to listen passively rather than to engage personally.

- Try not to interrupt, judge, or minimize anyone's comments or input.
- Remember that you are not expected to be the expert or have all the answers. Acknowledge that all of you are on this journey together, with the Holy Spirit as your leader and guide. If issues or questions arise that you don't feel equipped to answer or handle, talk with the pastor or a staff member at your church.
- Encourage good discussion, but don't be timid about calling time on a particular question and moving ahead. Part of your responsibility is to keep the group on track. If you decide to spend extra time on a given question or activity, consider skipping or spending less time on another question or activity in order to stay on schedule.
- Try to end on time. If you are running over, give members the opportunity to leave if they need to. Then wrap up as quickly as you can.
- Be prepared for some women to want to hang out and talk at the end. If you need everyone to leave by a certain time, communicate this at the beginning of the session. If you are meeting in a church during regularly scheduled activities or have arranged for childcare, be sensitive to the agreed-upon ending time.
- Thank the women for coming, and let them know you're looking forward to seeing them next time.

Introductory Session

Leader Prep

Materials Needed

- *Romans* DVD and DVD player or equipment to stream the video online
- Stick-on nametags and markers (optional)
- Index cards (optional—Prayer Requests)
- *Romans* participant workbooks to purchase or distribute

Session Outline

Note: Refer to the format templates on page 8 in this Leader Guide for suggested time allotments. The regular session outline has been modified for this optional introductory session, which is 60 minutes long.

Welcome

Offer a word of welcome to the group. If time allows and you choose to provide food, invite the women to enjoy refreshments and fellowship. (Groups meeting for 60 minutes may want to have a time for food and fellowship before the official start time.) Be sure to watch the clock and move to the All Play icebreaker at the appropriate time.

All Play

Ask each group member to share a little about herself—name, interests, how many Bible studies she's been a part of, and so on.

Distribute the participant workbooks, and then have the group turn to the introduction (page 9). Ask volunteers to read one paragraph each until you've read through the first section of the introduction (up to "Options for Study"). Then point out the different options for study (pages 10–11) and encourage each woman to prayerfully decide what level of study she would like to complete. Decide ahead of time whether you will encourage all of the ladies in your group to consider reading the online "Digging Deeper" articles.

Prayer/Video

Ask God to prepare the group to be receptive and hear His voice. Play the "Introductory Session" video. Let the women know that this information is also provided as Introductory Background in their workbooks (pages 12–13), so it is not necessary for them to take notes.

Discuss:

- What do you already know about the church at Rome? What insights and/or questions did this introductory video raise for you?
- How can knowing more about the lives of the original audience for this letter help you to interpret and apply it?
- Read Romans 1:16-17 together. How is this good news in your life today?
- What do you hope to learn or gain from this study?

Prayer Requests

End by inviting group members to share prayer requests and pray for one another. Use index cards, popcorn prayer, or another prayer technique included in "Tips for Tackling Five Common Challenges" (pages 18–19 in this Leader Guide) to lead this time with intentionality and sensitivity.

Session 1

Good News About Faith

Romans 1–3

Leader Prep

Memory Verses

[16]For I am not ashamed of this Good News about Christ. It is the power of God at work, saving everyone who believes—the Jew first and also the Gentile. [17]This Good News tells us how God makes us right in his sight. This is accomplished from start to finish by faith. As the Scriptures say, "It is through faith that a righteous person has life."

(Romans 1:16-17)

Materials Needed

- Romans DVD and DVD player
- Stick-on nametags and markers (optional)
- Index cards or sticky notes (optional—Scriptures and Prayer Requests)

Session Outline

Note: Refer to the format templates on page 8 in this Leader Guide for suggested time allotments.

Welcome

Offer a word of welcome to the group. If time allows and you choose to provide food, invite the women to enjoy refreshments and fellowship. (Groups meeting for 60 minutes may want to have a time for food and fellowship before the official start time.) Be sure to watch the clock and move to the All Play icebreaker at the appropriate time.

All Play

Ask each group member to respond briefly to the following prompt:

- Which small appliance (something you plug in) have you used the most this week?

After everyone has shared, say something like this:

- Whether you used your toaster oven or curling iron more frequently this week, it needed to be plugged in so that it would work. We began this week talking about God's power. He is powerful, but sometimes we feel powerless. We found in our study that through faith we can connect with our powerful God. Let's pray to Him as we get started today.

Prayer/Video

Ask God to prepare the group to receive His Word and hear His voice. Play the video for Week 1. Invite participants to complete the "Video Viewer Guide" for Week 1 in the participant workbook as they watch (page 45). (Answers are provided on page 200.)

Group Discussion

Video Discussion Questions

- Have you ever been lost, unsure of where you were? What were some of the emotions you encountered?
- What masks that were mentioned in the video could you relate with? What are some other kinds of masks that we put on to find identity?
- The good news is not just information but an invitation. Would anyone be willing to share when they first responded to that invitation?
- How has God's kindness in your life led you to turn away from sin?

Participant Workbook Discussion Questions

Note: Page references are provided for those questions that relate to questions or activities in the participant workbook.

Before you begin, invite volunteers to look up the following Scriptures and to be prepared to read them aloud when called upon. You might want to write each of the Scripture references on a separate index card or sticky note that you can hand out.

Scriptures:

Romans 1:8-15
Romans 1:16-17
Romans 1:21-25
Romans 2:25-29
Romans 3:21-31

Day 1: *The Power*

- What spiritual posture did you identify in your life as you begin this study? Are you resigned, indifferent, curious, expectant, or something else? (page 15)
- Have someone read aloud Romans 1:8-15. Invite the women to share the thoughts or questions that stood out to them from these verses. (page 17)
- Have someone read aloud Romans 1:16-17. The Greek word for "power" is related to our word for "dynamite." How have you seen God's life-changing power in your life recently or in the past? Whether or not you have seen the "dynamite" power of the good news of Jesus recently in your life, how would you like to see His power working in your life in the days and weeks ahead? (pages 19– 20) How would you like God to change you spiritually?

Day 2: *The Great Exchange*

- What are some glimpses you've seen of God in creation recently? (page 22)
- Have someone read aloud Romans 1:21-25. How have you seen the progression that leads to this great exchange of truth for a lie played out in the world? (page 23)

- What questions or insights did today's lesson about God's reaction toward sin bring? What helps you to embrace both God's love and God's holiness?

Day 3: The Secret Life

- What was going on in the church in Rome that warranted Paul distinguishing between the Jewish and Gentile believers? How did our study on Day 3 help you to have a better understanding of Paul's words directed to these two groups?
- What would you identify as Paul's main message from Romans 2:1-15? (page 31)
- How can we in the church today acknowledge distinctions while still focusing on commonalities? (page 32)

Day 4: A Changed Heart

- How is God calling you to "take a look" at your own heart and life as you read Romans rather than think about how it applies to others?
- Have someone read aloud Romans 2:25-29. What are some Christian practices or traditions that people sometimes elevate above the heart behind it? (page 35)
- What truths stood out to you from our three areas of study today: Take A Look, Give Up, and Get Real? (page 37)

Day 5: Bad News and Good News

- Why is it important to understand the bad news in order to appreciate the good news? Give some examples.
- Have someone read aloud Romans 3:21-31. Share how you would explain the message found in these verses to a person who had never heard it before. (page 40)
- As you filled in the blanks on page 42 with your name, acknowledging that you have been declared righteous and have been freed from slavery to sin, what encouragement did this exercise bring in the midst of any bad news you have encountered this week?

Optional "Digging Deeper" Summary (for a session longer than 60 minutes)

Ask a group member ahead of time to review the "Digging Deeper" article for Week 1, "The Saints" (see AbingdonWomen.com/Romans), and to be prepared to share with the group what stood out to her, either summarizing insights or reading a few sentences. Allow 2–3 minutes for this sharing.

Optional Group Activity *(for a session longer than 60 minutes)*

Divide into smaller groups or pairs to review the "Weekly Wrap Up" (pages 43–44). Ask small groups to share and discuss how they will put into practice something they learned from their readings this week.

Prayer Requests

Invite the group members to share prayer requests and pray for one another. Use index cards or sticky notes, popcorn prayer, or another prayer technique included in "Tips for Tackling Five Common Challenges" (pages 18–19 in this Leader Guide) to lead this time with intentionality and sensitivity.

Session 2

Good News About Hope

Romans 4–5

Leader Prep

Memory Verse

But God demonstrates his own love for us in this: While we were still sinners, Christ died for us.

(Romans 5:8 NIV)

Materials Needed

- *Romans* DVD and DVD player
- Stick-on nametags and markers (optional)
- Index cards or sticky notes (optional—Scriptures and Prayer Requests)

Session Outline

Note: Refer to the format templates on page 8 in this Leader Guide for suggested time allotments.

Welcome

Offer a word of welcome to the group. If time allows and you choose to provide food, invite the women to enjoy refreshments and fellowship. (Groups meeting for 60 minutes may want to have a time for food and fellowship before the official start time.) Be sure to watch the clock and move to the All Play icebreaker at the appropriate time.

All Play

Ask each group member to respond briefly to the following prompt. Read aloud or paraphrase:

- This week we explored the good news about hope. At times we hope for small things like good weather or a close parking spot. Other times we hope for more significant things like grandchildren or a new career opportunity. What is something that you've hoped for that actually happened?

Prayer/Video

Ask God to prepare the group to receive His Word and hear His voice. Play the video for Week 2. Invite participants to complete the "Video Viewer Guide" for Week 2 in the participant workbook as they watch (page 75). (Answers are provided on page 200.)

Group Discussion

Video Discussion Questions

- How has hope been an anchor in your life recently?
- As you reflect on your spiritual journey, what individuals have served as examples of those who have a secure anchor in Christ?
- How does knowing that God can bring the dead back to life and create new things out of nothing speak to your current prayer requests?
- Have any of your past or current trials led you to hope through perseverance or character development? Share a little about this process for you personally.

Participant Workbook Discussion Questions

Note: Page references are provided for those questions that relate to questions or activities in the participant workbook.

Before you begin, invite volunteers to look up the following Scriptures and to be prepared to read them aloud when called upon. You might want to write each of the Scripture references on a separate index card or sticky note that you can hand out.

Scriptures:

Genesis 12:2-3
Romans 4:1-5
Romans 5:1-5
Romans 5:6-11
Romans 5:12-21

Day 1: *Hope in a Family*

- Have someone read aloud Genesis 12:2-3. How does the blessing given to Abraham relate to you and me? (page 48)
- Have someone read aloud Romans 4:1-5. What do these verses tell us that God uses as the basis of whether we are counted as righteous? (page 47)
- Are you now or have you ever been connected to a larger family of believers? If so, how has being part of a local church body impacted your faith (either negatively or positively)? (page 49)
- We learned that those who choose to follow Jesus are not meant to live the Christian life in isolation. In what ways might God be calling you to deeper connections with your faith community? What suggestions or ideas did you check on page 50?

Day 2: *Against All Hope*

- What is something you are hoping for right now? (page 51) Why is it important that our faith is built on God's promises?
- What are some of God's promises that you have chosen to stand on even when they haven't "felt" true in your life and circumstances? (page 53)
- According to today's lesson, what is the difference between faith and hope?

Day 3: *Hope That Does Not Disappoint*

- Can you think of a time when you were looking forward to something but ended up disappointed in the way it turned out? (page 58)
- Have someone read aloud Romans 5:1-5. What challenges are you facing right now that have the potential to strengthen your hope muscle? (page 61)
- What are some things you have put your hope in that have led to disappointment?

- Have someone read aloud Romans 5:5 once again. How have you experienced the Holy Spirit filling your heart with the love of God? Was it during a season of difficulty or a season of celebration?

Day 4: Hope in Christ's Life

- Have someone read aloud Romans 5:6-11. What stands out to you from these verses?
- How does Romans 5:8, our memory verse this week, encourage you as think about Christ's sacrifice on your behalf?
- What aspect of friendship do you most relate to in your relationship with God right now? (page 65)
- Romans 5:10 says that we were restored by the death of Christ and saved by the life of Christ. What do you think this means? (page 66)
- Is there an area in your life and ministry where your internal questions need to change? (page 67)

Day 5: Hope in the Second Adam

- Have someone read aloud Romans 5:12-21. What books, movies, or real life stories that contain a redemptive theme come to mind for you as you think about this passage? (page 71)
- How does this good news of God's grace give you hope personally? (page 71)
- As you look back over the entire week, what truths from Romans 4–5 have resonated most with you, and why?

Optional "Digging Deeper" Summary (for a session longer than 60 minutes)

Ask a group member ahead of time to review the "Digging Deeper" article for Week 2, "Covenant Signs" (see AbingdonWomen.com/Romans), and to be prepared to share with the group what stood out to her, either summarizing insights or reading a few sentences. Allow 2–3 minutes for this sharing.

Optional Group Activity (for a session longer than 60 minutes)

Divide into smaller groups or pairs to review the "Weekly Wrap Up" (page 74). Ask small groups to share and discuss how they will put into practice something they learned from their readings this week.

Prayer Requests

Invite the group members to share prayer requests and pray for one another. Use index cards or sticky notes, popcorn prayer, or another prayer technique included in "Tips for Tackling Five Common Challenges" (pages 18–19 in this Leader Guide) to lead this time with intentionality and sensitivity.

Session 3

Good News About Daily Life

Romans 6–8

Leader Prep

Memory Verse

And I am convinced that nothing can ever separate us from God's love. Neither death nor life, neither angels nor demons, neither our fears for today nor our worries about tomorrow—not even the powers of hell can separate us from God's love.

(Romans 8:38)

Materials Needed

- *Romans* DVD and DVD player
- Stick-on nametags and markers (optional)
- Index cards or sticky notes (optional—Scriptures and Prayer Requests)

Session Outline

Note: *Refer to the format templates on page 8 in this Leader Guide for suggested time allotments.*

Welcome

Offer a word of welcome to the group. If time allows and you choose to provide food, invite the women to enjoy refreshments and fellowship. (Groups meeting

for 60 minutes may want to have a time for food and fellowship before the official start time.) Be sure to watch the clock and move to the All Play icebreaker at the appropriate time.

All Play

Ask each group member to respond briefly to the following prompt. Read aloud or paraphrase:

- This week we talked about daily life. Sometimes when things become familiar, they are not as significant as they once were. What is something that hangs on a wall in your home that you see often without really thinking about it?

After everyone has shared, say:

- The good news about Jesus may be something we've seen and heard many times, but we don't want to lose the wonder of it in our daily lives.

Prayer/Video

Ask God to prepare the group to receive His Word and hear His voice. Play the video for Week 3. Invite participants to complete the "Video Viewer Guide" for Week 3 in the participant workbook as they watch (page 105). (Answers are provided on page 200.)

Group Discussion

Video Discussion Questions

- How have you found Jesus to be a gentle shepherd in your life?
- What was your reaction to Eugene Peterson's illustration of spiritual tourists and pilgrims? Where do you find yourself on your own spiritual pilgrimage—valley, mountaintop, or plateau?
- What helps you keep your "gospel headphones" on so that your spiritual activity flows out of your response to the good news?

Participant Workbook Discussion Questions

Note: Page references are provided for those questions that relate to questions or activities in the participant workbook.

Before you begin, invite volunteers to look up the following Scriptures and to be prepared to read them aloud when called upon. You might want to write each

of the Scripture references on a separate index card or sticky note that you can hand out.

Scriptures:

Romans 6:1-11
Romans 6:12-14
Romans 7:1-6
Romans 7:14-25
Romans 8:1
Romans 8:5-8
Romans 8:9-17
Romans 8:18-25

Day 1: Independence Day

- Have someone read aloud Romans 6:1-11. How do these verses ring true—or conflict—with your daily battle with sin? (page 78)
- Have someone read aloud Romans 6:12-14. As you think about these instructions, what are some practices that help you live out these commands? In other words, what helps you *not* to give in to sin—whether the battle is in your mind, words, attitudes, or actions? (page 79)
- How can we experience freedom from sin by submitting to God? Invite participants to share a personal example as they are willing.

Day 2: The Failure of Legalism

- How have you encountered the tension between license and legalism when it comes to God's truth?
- Have someone read aloud Romans 7:1-6. What in these verses stands out to you?
- How would you explain the purpose of the law based on our lesson today? (page 86)

Day 3: Struggling but Not Condemned

- Have someone read aloud Romans 7:14-25. As you read Paul's description of the war within, can you relate with his struggle? In what ways? (page 89)
- Have someone read aloud Romans 8:1. How does this verse encourage you?
- How would *you* summarize the big idea for today? (page 91)

Day 4: Surrendering Control

- Have someone read aloud Romans 8:5-8. What are some words that come to your mind as you think about the Holy Spirit? (page 93)
- Have someone read aloud Romans 8:9-17. What are some further insights we find in these verses regarding the Holy Spirit? (Refer to your notes on page 93.)
- Based on the Scriptures we've read in Romans today, what changes would you like to see in your relationship with the Holy Spirit? (page 94)

Day 5: Future Glory

- Share one or two challenges you have faced or are facing that have been difficult. (page 97)
- Have someone read aloud Romans 8:18-25. How do these truths affect your posture toward your current struggles today? (page 99)
- Have you been able to see something challenging work together for good in your life? (page 100)
- As you reflect on our study of Romans 6–8 this week, what are some of your biggest takeaways?

Optional "Digging Deeper" Summary *(for a session longer than 60 minutes)*

Ask a group member ahead of time to review the "Digging Deeper" article for Week 3, "Dive" (see AbingdonWomen.com/Romans), and to be prepared to share with the group what stood out to her, either summarizing insights or reading a few sentences. Allow 2–3 minutes for this sharing.

Optional Group Activity *(for a session longer than 60 minutes)*

Divide into smaller groups or pairs to review the "Weekly Wrap Up" on (pages 103–104). Ask small groups to share and discuss how they will put into practice something they learned from their readings this week.

Prayer Requests

Invite the group members to share prayer requests and pray for one another. Use index cards or sticky notes, popcorn prayer, or another prayer technique included in "Tips for Tackling Five Common Challenges" (pages 18–19 in the Leader Guide) to lead this time with intentionality and sensitivity.

Session 4

Good News About God's Plan

Romans 9–11

Leader Prep

Memory Verses

[9]*If you openly declare that Jesus is Lord and believe in your heart that God raised him from the dead, you will be saved.* [10]*For it is by believing in your heart that you are made right with God, and it is by openly declaring your faith that you are saved.*

(Romans 10:9-10)

Materials Needed

- Romans DVD and DVD player
- Stick-on nametags and markers (optional)
- Index cards or sticky notes (optional—Scriptures and Prayer Requests)

Session Outline

Note: *Refer to the format templates on page 8 in this Leader Guide for suggested time allotments.*

Welcome

Offer a word of welcome to the group. If time allows and you choose to provide food, invite the women to enjoy refreshments and fellowship. (Groups meeting

for 60 minutes may want to have a time for food and fellowship before the official start time.) Be sure to watch the clock and move to the All Play icebreaker at the appropriate time.

All Play

Ask each group member to respond briefly to the following prompt. Read aloud or paraphrase:

- What are your plans for dinner tonight?

- Whether you are eating out, warming up leftovers, preparing a meal, or have no idea about dinner tonight—you will likely consume some food in one way or another. When it comes to God's plan for His people, which is our topic of study this week, we can rest assured that He isn't winging it like we sometimes do with dinner plans!

Prayer/Video

Ask God to prepare the group to receive His Word and hear His voice. Play the video for Week 4. Invite participants to complete the "Video Viewer Guide" for Week 4 in the participant workbook as they watch (page 134). (Answers are provided on page 200.)

Group Discussion

Video Discussion Questions

- If you zoom out for a bigger picture perspective of your life, where and how might God be at work?
- How did you first hear the good news about Jesus coming to earth, dying on the cross, and rising again for the sin of the world?
- When did you first believe in your heart and confess with your mouth the good news about Christ?
- What are some of the best ways you've encountered to share the good news about Jesus with others?

Participant Workbook Discussion Questions

Note: Page references are provided for those questions that relate to questions or activities in the participant workbook.

Before you begin, invite volunteers to look up the following Scriptures and to be prepared to read them aloud when called upon. You might want to write each

of the Scripture references on a separate index card or sticky note that you can hand out.

Scriptures:

Romans 9:30-33
Romans 10:9-10
Romans 10:14-15
Romans 10:16-21
Romans 11:1-10
Romans 11:22
Romans 11:29
Romans 11:33-36

Day 1: *Overlapping Truths*

- Have group members review Romans 9:6-29 on their own silently. Then ask: What do you think is the main point Paul is trying to make in this discourse? (page 108)
- After learning briefly about Calvinism and Arminianism, what are your thoughts on the issue of predestination and free will, or what questions do you have? (page 111)
- Have someone read aloud Romans 9:30-33. What stumbling blocks might be keeping you from trusting God more? (page 111)

Day 2: *Relationships Over Rules*

- Have someone read aloud Romans 10:9-10. How would you summarize these verses in your own words? (page 115)
- If someone asked you to explain the gospel in a few sentences, what would you say?
- Who was influential in helping you gain clarity about the meaning of Christ's death and resurrection? (page 117)
- If you have confessed with your mouth and believed in your heart that Jesus Christ is Lord, briefly describe that experience. Feel free to be as specific or as general as you wish. (page 117)

Day 3: *Beautiful Feet*

- What did you say is your current favorite personal footwear? (page 119)

- Have someone read aloud Romans 10:14-15. Who has invited you to church, Bible study, or some other gathering that led you to grow in faith? (page 120)
- What good news have you shared with others lately? (page 121)
- Ask a participant to read aloud Romans 10:16-21. How does faith come according to verse 17? (page 123) What are some tangible ways that you hear God's Word on a regular basis? How does your faith grow as you hear? Is there a difference in hearing and listening?

Day 4: The Family Plan

- Have someone read Romans 11:1-10. What did you write as your own definition for grace based on what you read (see verses 5 and 6)? (page 125)
- How have you experienced God's favor in your life lately? (page 126)
- Have someone read aloud Romans 11:22. God's family plan includes a gracious invitation to all who will believe Him. What two qualities of God does Paul identify in this verse? (page 127)
- Where is God asking you to trust His plan in your life right now? (page 128)

Day 5: Mysterious Plans

- Have someone read Romans 11:29. Paul is speaking of God's covenant promises made with Israel; but how do you think the concept that God's gifts and call can never be withdrawn applies in our lives as believers today? (page 130)
- Have someone read Romans 11:33-36 and discuss some of God's qualities. (page 131)
- What is something God has given you that you are thankful for right now? (page 131)
- As you reflect on our study of Romans 9–11 this week, what truths or verses have resonated most with you?

Optional "Digging Deeper" Summary (for a session longer than 60 minutes)

Ask a group member ahead of time to review the "Digging Deeper" article for Week 4, "The Romans Road" (see AbingdonWomen.com/Romans), and to be prepared to share with the group what stood out to her, either summarizing insights or reading a few sentences. Allow 2–3 minutes for this sharing.

Optional Group Activity *(for a session longer than 60 minutes)*

Divide into smaller groups or pairs to review the "Weekly Wrap Up" on (page 133). Ask small groups to share and discuss how they will put into practice something they learned from their readings this week.

Prayer Requests

Invite the group members to share prayer requests and pray for one another. Use index cards or sticky notes, popcorn prayer, or another prayer technique included in "Tips for Tackling Five Common Challenges" (page 15 in this Leader Guide) to lead this time with intentionality and sensitivity.

Session 5

Good News About Relationships

Romans 12–14

Leader Prep

Memory Verses

[1]And so, dear brothers and sisters, I plead with you to give your bodies to God because of all he has done for you. Let them be a living and holy sacrifice—the kind he will find acceptable. This is truly the way to worship him. [2]Don't copy the behavior and customs of this world, but let God transform you into a new person by changing the way you think. Then you will learn to know God's will for you, which is good and pleasing and perfect.

(Romans 12:1-2)

Materials Needed

- *Romans* DVD and DVD player
- Stick-on nametags and markers (optional)
- Index cards or sticky notes (optional—Scriptures and Prayer Requests)

Session Outline

Note: Refer to the format templates on page 8 in this Leader Guide for suggested time allotments.

Welcome

Offer a word of welcome to the group. If time allows and you choose to provide food, invite the women to enjoy refreshments and fellowship. (Groups meeting for 60 minutes may want to have a time for food and fellowship before the official start time.) Be sure to watch the clock and move to the All Play icebreaker at the appropriate time.

All Play

Ask each group member to respond briefly to the following prompt:

- When was the last time you either were in a photo booth or posed for a professional picture?

After everyone shares, say:

- Posing is great for photo booths, but bad for relationships. We'll talk more about loving and honoring others in our time together today.

Prayer/Video

Ask God to prepare the group to receive His Word and hear His voice. Play the video for Week 5. Invite participants to complete the "Video Viewer Guide" for Week 5 in the participant workbook as they watch (page 165). (Answers are provided on page 200.)

Group Discussion

Video Discussion Questions

- In what area of your life would you like to know God's pleasing and perfect will?
- What people do you sense the Lord calling you to truly love without pretense?
- What preferences or convictions of yours have changed over time?
- What choices can you make this week to honor others?

Participant Workbook Discussion Questions

Note: Page references are provided for those questions that relate to questions or activities in the participant workbook.

Before you begin, invite volunteers to look up the following Scriptures and to be prepared to read them aloud when called upon. You might want to write each

of the Scripture references on a separate index card or sticky note that you can hand out.

Scriptures:

Romans 12:1-2
Romans 12:3-8
Romans 12:9-21
Romans 13:1-7
Romans 13:8-10
Romans 13:11-14
Romans 14:1-9

Day 1: *Lasting Change*

- Have someone read aloud Romans 12:1-2. How did you summarize Paul's instructions to believers in your own words? (page 138)
- In your opinion, what are some of the worldly patterns and behaviors that we must not conform to? (There are many answers; just pick two or three.) (page 139)
- What are some practical ways that you renew your mind to allow Christ to bring change (metamorphosis) in your life? (page 139)
- After reflecting on Romans 12:1-2, what type of changes would you like to implement when it comes to your thought life? (page 141)

Day 2: *Bullfrogs and Butterflies*

- In what area of your life would you like to see transformation right now? How would change in this area impact your closest relationships? (page 142)
- Have someone read aloud Romans 12:3-8. What might a changed person's life reveal according to these verses? (page 143)
- What is one spiritual gift you either know or suspect you have, and how are you using it to benefit others within the body of Christ? (page 143)
- How have you experienced spiritual renewal and personal growth as you've used your gifts to serve others? (page 144)
- Have someone read aloud Romans 12:9-21. Which of these commands stood out most to you? (pages 144–145)

Day 3: Love and Respect

- Have someone read aloud Romans 13:1-7. What is your initial reaction to these verses? (page 148)
- What are some practical ways that, as believers, we can honor our governing authorities? (page 150)
- Have someone read aloud Romans 13:8-10. How would you summarize Paul's message about love in a few sentences? (page 151)
- I wonder how the Lord is calling you to love right now. What is one way you can max out your love credit card today? (page 151)

Day 4: Belief and Behavior

- Have someone read aloud Romans 13:11-14. What thoughts or questions do you have about the roles of belief and behavior in regard to salvation? (page 153)
- Have you struggled with any apathy, boredom, or distraction in your faith lately? If so, how? What are some things that wake you up to the priority of faith and action? (page 155)
- Read together the verses on page 156. What are the truths related to these words or phrases that resonate with you? (page 157)

Day 5: Into the Gray

- What are some gray areas for us Christians that come to your mind? (page 158)
- Have someone read aloud Romans 14:1-9. How did you boil down the core message of Paul's teaching in one sentence? (page 159)
- Where is the Lord calling you to accept someone else (who might see things differently than you in some area) right now? (page 159)
- As you reflect on our study of Romans 12–14 this week, what concepts have stood out most to you?

Optional "Digging Deeper" Summary (for a session longer than 60 minutes)

Ask a group member ahead of time to review the "Digging Deeper" article for Week 5, "Come to the Altar" (see AbingdonWomen.com/Romans), and to be prepared to share with the group what stood out to her, either summarizing insights or reading a few sentences. Allow 2–3 minutes for this sharing.

Optional Group Activity *(for a session longer than 60 minutes)*

Divide into smaller groups or pairs to review the "Weekly Wrap Up" on (pages 163–164). Ask small groups to share and discuss how they will put into practice something they learned from their readings this week.

Prayer Requests

Invite the group members to share prayer requests and pray for one another. Use index cards or sticky notes, popcorn prayer, or another prayer technique included in "Tips for Tackling Five Common Challenges" (pages 18–19 in this Leader Guide) to lead this time with intentionality and sensitivity.

Session 6

Good News About Eternity

Romans 15–16

Leader Prep

Memory Verse

The God of peace will soon crush Satan under your feet. May the grace of our Lord Jesus be with you.

(Romans 16:20)

Materials Needed

- *Romans* DVD and DVD player
- Stick-on nametags and markers (optional)
- Blank cardstock bookmarks and gel pens (optional—Group Activity)
- Index cards or sticky notes (optional—Scriptures and Prayer Requests)

Session Outline

Note: *Refer to the format templates on page 8 in this Leader Guide for suggested time allotments.*

Welcome

Offer a word of welcome to the group. If time allows and you choose to provide food, invite the women to enjoy refreshments and fellowship. (Groups meeting

for 60 minutes may want to have a time for food and fellowship before the official start time.) Be sure to watch the clock and move to the All Play icebreaker at the appropriate time.

All Play

Ask each group member to respond briefly to the following prompt. Read aloud or paraphrase:

- What is the last thing you made in a blender?

- Whether it was a smoothie, soup, or drink, you likely blended several different ingredients together to create tastes and textures that complement each other. This week we'll talk more about harmony in Christ and God's eternal plan for His people.

Prayer/Video

Ask God to prepare the group to receive His Word and hear His voice. Play the video for Week 6. Invite participants to complete the "Video Viewer Guide" for Week 6 in the participant workbook as they watch (page 198). (Answers are provided on page 200.)

Group Discussion

Video Discussion Questions

- Of all the props on the stage, which one do you think you will remember in the months and/or years ahead when you reflect on Romans?
- How does knowing that your suffering has an expiration date bring you particular encouragement today?
- How can you value people above stuff this week?
- What would it look like for you to be a "there you are" rather than a "here I am" person in your sphere of influence?

Participant Workbook Discussion Questions

Note: Page references are provided for those questions that relate to questions or activities in the participant workbook.

Before you begin, invite volunteers to look up the following Scriptures and to be prepared to read them aloud when called upon. You might want to write each of the Scripture references on a separate index card or sticky note that you can hand out.

Scriptures:

> Romans 15:1-7
> Romans 15:13
> Romans 15:14-22
> Romans 15:30-33

Day 1: Harmony, Hope, and the Holy Spirit

- Ask someone to define *justification, sanctification,* and *glorification* in their own words.
- Have someone read aloud Romans 15:1-7. What do these verses say about harmony? What are some practical ways you can take these teachings to heart as you accept other believers who have different opinions than you do? (page 170)
- Have someone read aloud Romans 15:13. What power does God say will help us abound in hope?

Day 2: Godly Confidence

- Can you identify a time in your life when you lacked confidence? Describe what comes to mind off the top of your head. (page 173)
- Have someone read aloud Romans 15:14-22. How can we know the difference between prideful ambition and godly goals as we seek to live confidently for Christ? (page 173)
- What are some of the things you've learned about God from our study of Romans that could bring someone confidence? (page 174)

Day 3: Travel Plans and Prayers

- What are some plans you are making for your next week, month, and year? (pages 180–181)
- Have someone read aloud Romans 15:30-33. What were some of the specific things Paul asked the church at Rome to pray for him? (page 181)
- From today's study, what takeaways do you have when it comes to making plans and allowing the Lord to direct your steps?

Day 4: Spiritual Friends

- Have someone read aloud Romans 16:1-16. What were some of the personal comments Paul made to his spiritual friends in Rome that stood out to you? (page 183)

- Share one of the people you wrote in the various categories of friends and mentors in your life who are similar to those Paul listed. (page 184)
- What steps is God calling you to take to be more intentional in forging spiritual friendships?

Day 5: Victory

- Have someone read aloud Romans 16:17-20. How did you summarize Paul's final appeal and encouragement to the church? (page 187)
- Now that we have studied Romans, how would you summarize the gospel message in a few sentences? (If you need help, look back at Romans 5:8.) (page 188)
- Have someone read aloud Romans 16:20. Whom does Paul say will be crushed? (page 188) How does this verse encourage you? (page 189)
- Have someone read aloud Romans 16:21-27. What does Paul say in verse 27? (page 189) As you reflect on our study of Romans, what has stood out to you? What did you star on the summary chart? (pages 190–195)

Optional "Digging Deeper" Summary *(for a session longer than 60 minutes)*

Ask a group member ahead of time to review the "Digging Deeper" article for Week 6, "Kissing Christians" (see AbingdonWomen.com/Romans), and to be prepared to share with the group what stood out to her, either summarizing insights or reading a few sentences. Allow 2–3 minutes for this sharing.

Optional Group Activity *(for a session longer than 60 minutes)*

To close your study, hand out blank cardstock bookmarks and set out some gel pens or colored pencils. Ask participants to reflect on the memory verses and main points they've studied over the last six weeks, and invite them to write a favorite memory verse, word, or quotation from a daily reading on their bookmarks. If you have time, ask some volunteers to share what they wrote and why.

Prayer Requests

Invite the group members to share prayer requests and pray for one another. Use index cards or sticky notes, popcorn prayer, or another prayer technique included in "Tips for Tackling Five Common Challenges" (pages 18–19 in this Leader Guide) to lead this time with intentionality and sensitivity. Give thanks for all that you have learned and experienced together, and ask God to help you share the good news you've studied with others in the coming weeks.

Digging Deeper
Week 1 Preview

The Saints

See AbingdonWomen.com/Romans for other "Digging Deeper" articles.

Most days I don't feel like a saint. I forget important things. I'm forever behind on laundry. I know I should pray more and give greater attention to the suffering going on in the world. I agree with God that I am a sinner in need of saving. Yet in the first few verses of Romans, we don't find Paul addressing the church as sinners. Instead he called them saints. What exactly did Paul mean when he called the believers at Rome *saints*? How does this word used in Scripture and in church history apply to believers today?

In Romans 1:7, Paul greets the church at Rome this way, "I am writing to all of you in Rome who are loved by God and are called to be his own holy people. May God our Father and the Lord Jesus Christ give you grace and peace." This same verse is translated in the English Standard Version, "To all those in Rome who are loved by God and *called to be saints*: Grace to you and peace from God our Father and the Lord Jesus Christ" (emphasis added). The King James, New King James, and New American Standard Versions also translate this verse using the word *saints*. The Greek word is *hagios*, which means, "a most holy thing; saint."[1] This word is used eighteen times in fifteen verses in the Book of Romans in reference to the law, the Scriptures, the Spirit of God, and also the people of God—the saints.[2]

By referring to the Christians at Rome as saints, Paul wasn't calling them virtuous or commending their behavior. Instead he was reminding them of their position before God. Saints are not a select few "super Christians" who are worthy of the title. Because Christ died for our sins, every believer has a new identity as a saint. We are holy, which means "set apart." Through Christ we are no longer separated from God but are cleansed of sin and viewed by God as holy.

We can explore our own identity in Christ by understanding how the title *saint* applies in the life of a believer. By calling believers saints, Paul highlighted their unity, value, and uniqueness as the people of God.

- **Unity.** Throughout the Book of Romans, Paul encourages the church to recognize Gentile Christians as part of God's family. Though the Jews have a history of relationship with God, Gentiles share equal ground at the foot of the cross. In the Old Testament the term *saints* is used less frequently (see Exodus 19:5-6; Leviticus 19:2; Deuteronomy 7:6). The Hebrew word for saint is *qadowsh*, which also means holy or set apart.[3] By calling all members of the Roman church saints, Paul is communicating to the Gentiles that they are as much a part of the people of God as Israel.

- **Value.** Because God views us as saints, we have confidence before God. He does not condemn us but sees us as worthy of the greatest sacrifice. He valued us enough to send His Son to die in our place so that we might be holy through Christ. So now we can attach value to ourselves, not with prideful achievement or good behavior but because God has set us apart as worthy to be loved. When we see ourselves as the saints we are, we can live and act out of our identity as those treasured by God.

- **Uniqueness.** By calling the people of the church at Rome saints, Paul also is reminding them that they are no longer like others around them. Because they are holy, they are set apart from the rest of the world. Their lives should look different from their neighbors, friends, and family members who do not know Christ. Hebrews 10:10 says, "For God's will was for us to be made holy by the sacrifice of the body of Jesus Christ, once for all time." We don't live differently by our own effort or hard work. Rather, out of the overflow of our love for Christ we can spend our time, treasures, and talents in a way that is not conformed to the pattern of this world but instead transformed by God's love (see Romans 12:1-2).

If you have given your life to Christ, then you are a saint—whether or not you feel like it today. By recognizing our identity as saints, we can find unity with other believers, value as those worthy of love, and uniqueness to live differently than the world around us.

Notes

1. *Hagios*, Strong's Concordance, https://www.biblestudytools.com/lexicons/greek/kjv/hagios .html. Accessed May 7, 2019.
2. *Hagios* in Romans, https://www.biblestudytools.com/kjv/passage/?q=ro+1:2;ro+1:7;ro+5:5; ro+7:12;ro+8:27;ro+9:1;ro+11:16;ro+12:1;ro+12:13;ro+14:17;ro+15:13;ro+15:16;ro+15:26;ro +16:2;ro+16:15;ro+16:16. Accessed May 7, 2019.
3. *Qadowsh*, Strong's Concordance, https://www.biblestudytools.com/lexicons/hebrew/kjv /qadowsh.html. Accessed May 7, 2019.

VIDEO VIEWER GUIDE ANSWERS

Week 1

trying / trusting

managed / suffering

kindness

Week 2

hope / Savior

God / said

Trials

Week 3

freedom / authority

struggle

godly / God

perspective

Week 4

sovereign plan

gospel

share

Week 5

vertical / horizontal

Posing

honor

Week 6

expiration date

right place

people / stuff

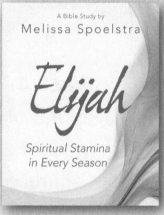
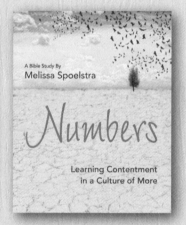

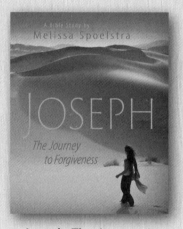
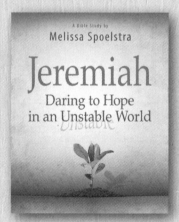